Poverty
Power Management
&
Development Leadership

Vol. 2

Remedy

By
Ramaswamy Thanu

Contents

"

1. Introduction

"So long as the millions live in hunger and ignorance, I hold every person a traitor who, having been educated at their expense pays not the least heed to them"
Swami Vivekananda

Poverty is a global phenomenon. The situation is depressing even after several measures been initiated and implemented by governments.

It is the author's conviction that leadership has a great and critical role in elimination of poverty. The theme of the book is developed linking poverty and leadership. The conclusion derives strength and support from the statements of eminent men like Robert McNamara, former President of World Bank, Nani Palkivala, eminent jurist and many others. The inadequacy of strong, competent and benevolent leadership accelerates poverty by denying and depriving the benefits of economic growth to the poor. Corruption, power mis-management and break down of law and order are evidences of weak leadership at various levels.

Deeply concerned about the pitiable condition of the poor and the lethargy of leadership at many levels of government and outside, the author in all humility, outlines a program of leadership development and social security for the poor.

The aim of the book is to plead before leaders, in all humility, to realize their role and to initiate positive and dynamic action for rapid economic growth in areas particularly relevant and beneficial to the poor.

The book is presented in two parts. Part 1 was already published. This second part deals with the concepts like power management, development leadership and character development in detail.

The author sincerely hopes that thousands of promising men in the country could be chosen for leadership training to serve a noble cause and for lasting results. The book may serve as an introduction to leadership development and an outline of an approach to the solution of the problem. Beyond this the author does not expect anything great to happen until the leaders assimilate the concepts and contents of the various chapters and act earnestly. If the target is well chosen, and the arrow fixed on the bow, the archer, assuming he is competent, releasing it will hit the target without fail. So for the best results the leader should be fully equipped, committed and trained. Such leadership alone can eliminate poverty.

2. Power Management

The government necessarily has to take the initiative in tackling problems of great social magnitude having far reaching implications. Economic planning becomes necessary. Such planning by the State implies concentration of power, and this power is the offspring of the political system. It is exercised through governmental leadership. So the task of the government becomes one of 'power management',

Having set objectives to benefit the people the nation's resources have to be deployed effectively. Technological advances do help to meet the growing demands of the population. But it is very difficult to increase the quantum of resources in the short term. So apart from conserving resources it is necessary to increase productivity.

A serious threat to productivity is unproductive employment. This arises from the pressures exerted by leaders, trade unions, and the unemployed for jobs. The economy needs productivity. Businessmen who work to attain this objective need support to lay off unproductive personnel. Necessary conditions for attaining this objective must be provided by the government. Under such conditions modernization programs have greater chance of success and there will be less resistance to change. The reduced labor strength is less likely to pose threats to the organization. It will be engaged in productive tasks, which are remunerative and satisfying. Organizations where such retrenchment takes place provide for social security benefits. They launch measures for higher productivity and efficiency. Those receiving such benefits can later take up jobs in the same organization or outside, in which case the benefits are discontinued. The retrenched personnel could be encouraged to become entrepreneurs. As an incentive the government will frame policies of financial assistance to them for starting small and medium enterprises. They can continue to get the benefits of social security for one year. This step has to be implemented boldly to relieve the pressure on jobs and to encourage self-employment.

Reward and performance must be matched and some objective criteria evolved for measuring them. Productivity research must be a compulsory feature in all areas of activity, especially in agriculture, education, health and law and order. This should aim at better community benefits. Prompt action by a few police men by way of deterrent action injuring or killing a single miscreant is preferable to the deployment of a large force achieving nothing and causing loss of several innocent lives later demoralizing the police force.

Democracy calls for people's participation. This will be freely forthcoming only if the masses are motivated to achieve something worthwhile. In making the individual more productive the most powerful agent is the force of motivation. It is here leadership can play an important role. When motivation - the force propelling an individual to excel his performance- is present and added to the factors of production economic progress is rapid and substantial. The task of institutions and organizations must be to motivate the human beings of concern to them. The reservoir of talent, which can motivate the masses into action, must be tapped along with other resources like land, labor, capital and enterprise.

Due to growing complexity of industrial organizations and the rising expectations of masses the limitations of material resources are felt. Resources management has become a complex activity. The two people oriented resources; labor and enterprise, have assumed importance and the quality of these two along with other factors of production determine the rate of economic growth. The most important resource required is enterprise- the ability to take calculated risks for creating wealth in the country. This talent, which is scarce, has to be developed and multiplied. Enterprising men are few and the labor force is large. There is generally a clash of interest between them. This results in wastage of precious and scarce resources. This loss can be minimized by the actions of the government. The latter has to give up the implicit policy of looking helplessly forcing the former to abdicate their right to manage industry. The condition will worsen if policies, like non-interference in labor disputes, are not discarded.

It is necessary to evaluate the employment potential of existing programs. To encourage employment and enterprise it is worth considering tax incentives based on employment. The government's labor polices framed with the intention of setting up an egalitarian society should not have the effect of freezing enterprise.

Leadership can succeed only when it utilizes the reservoir of motivation. Fortunately India has a glorious heritage where spirituality acts as a motivating force. In the past this helped considerably to develop supra ordinary goals and made people achievement oriented. Great national leaders like Mahatma Gandhi belonged to that category.

It is essential that motivational economics gains importance. The core of this theory lies in utilizing governmental power and spirituality as motivating tools. Apart from propelling the masses to achieve excellence they also help to curtail unnecessary low priority needs thereby relieving pressure on resources.

This is the new economics for economic development particularly for poverty alleviation. It is doubtful whether investment alone can bring prosperity. Employment alone is not indicative of the level of prosperity. This becomes explicit when we see the prevalence of a large force of unproductive labor in different categories in many organizations. Neither investment nor employment can provide the lever to alleviate poverty. Motivation, which deserves serious consideration as a prime resource, will provide the strength to alleviate poverty.

The role of the State will be to generate opportunities so that individuals and institutions are motivated to seize and realize them, thereby increasing employment and output. The State will concentrate only on those areas directly required to be under its control for strategic reasons. It will enter other areas of economic activity only when individuals and institutions do not have the strength, competence and resources to undertake such ventures. Even here, it will try to pass on the ownership and management of such activities to private organizations gradually. This will lighten the burden of the State and save and spare its resources for more important and worthwhile projects.

Undoubtedly the leadership of a country at various levels with the help of the machinery at its disposal is responsible for achieving economic progress. In a country with socialistic goals the government bestows on itself immense powers. Here it will be of use and interest to consider the concept of power along with its implications. Power is the invisible feature that makes it obligatory on citizens or agencies in administration, to act as per the dictates of the Executive in the national interest. It helps to improve the quality of life in the country.

Leadership within the government wields considerable power, which has great potential for good or bad. Power is the essential attribute of a government. It has to be used for achieving economic progress. Thus the function of the government becomes one of effective 'power management'.

The administrative system with its various hierarchies represents the power network controlling the source and flow of power required by the thousands of 'power centers'. These 'power centers' are manned by officials for translating into action the objectives of a welfare state. Power is also derived from outside the official power structure. Various individuals and sections of people have power lying dormant in them and this can be tapped with advantage. For the individual official at the 'power centre' his competence, skill, knowledge of the situation, its obstacle potential, ability to assess the strength of the interferences, and strategies to develop and conserve power, are all decisive factors in effective power utilization. In addition there are two important assets, which considerably help to develop power and to prevent 'power erosion'. These are discipline and motivation at all levels in the power hierarchy.

The power mechanism of the government has three wings. They are the Executive, Legislature and the Judiciary. The actions of these elements have a definite impact on the degree of success for economic development. Primarily the test for successful 'power management' will be whether the actions of these three have helped to increase productivity, the income flow of the economically weaker sections, to motivate people to work towards achieving social and economic justice and to strengthen the value systems conducive to economic growth.

Apart from these objectives the following principles will have to be observed by all agencies and leaders concerned.

- 'Power centers' will be motivated to excel in their performance and contribute to national prosperity
- 'Power centers' will increase their competence on a regular basis
- All sections of society will be motivated to excel their performance in the national interest
- Law and order will be maintained at any cost
- Power will be used as a tool for motivating all sections of the community
- Power will be used to curb activities of harmful consequences to the community
- Power will be used to get the best results from the community's resources
- Power will be used to promote activities of positive benefits to the community
- Privileged sections of society will have a specific role in ensuring social and economic justice
- Productivity will be encouraged
- Some of the supporting objectives required are:
- To use the tax system as a motivating tool for economic justice
- To define the role of the State as that to create opportunities for advancement of its citizens

- To give priority to the welfare of the unorganized masses will receive priority
- To avoid overlapping of functions and responsibilities of 'power centers'
- To determine the nature of legislative and judicial support required
- To determine the power channel and structure appropriate to discharging the government's functions
- To determine the power mix i.e., written, discretionary, legal cover, enactments etc.
- To increase competence of persons holding various 'power centers' and of those directly under the charge of each 'power centre'.
- To locate obstacles and constraints in the exercise of power and to remove them
- To locate power leakages and to plug them
- To look for source of power within and outside the power hierarchy and to make effective use of it discreetly for achieving power objectives
- To strengthen weak points
- To take the initiative for solving a problem by taking orders from the situation
- To recognize values are vital for progress.
- To remember violence in any form will be put down
- To review the power needs of the various 'power centers' at regular intervals and take corrective action promptly

The task of the government does not merely stop with deploying its power to get the best results from its resources. It has to recognize that the Opposition has enormous power because of its hold on the masses.

Like the various 'power centers' with power vested in them, the leadership at various levels constituting the Opposition has colossal power concealed in it. As long as the government in power taps this strength of the Opposition and diverts its energies for economic growth chances of such programs becoming successful are greater. Such an approach becomes impossible if the Opposition does not share the responsibility. This is more so if there are numerous opposition parties who are keen not to have any unanimity of approach except to topple down the government. Stalling parliamentary proceedings nonstop for over three weeks is not a healthy way of promoting economic progress.

The success of 'power management' depends on how effectively the power mechanism functions and how swiftly the various elements in the process work to conserve, develop, and build up power for attaining national objectives. Any lapse at any stage can work havoc on the power mechanism and cause break down of law and order. Deterioration in law and order weakens the power mechanism and makes it more ineffective thus thwarting progress.

Power structures constantly face challenges from within and without. There is need to identify the challenges, realize their implications and to deploy the power mechanism for corrective action. Orders have to be dictated by the situation and not by the individuals. The hierarchy is only to view the situation in its proper perspective and to issue commands when absolutely necessary. Inadequacies in 'power centers' should be met by transferring power to those points. Agitations threaten the power structure. Any delay in action paralyses it in such a manner that the agitators usurp power by sheer force of numbers and force the official 'power centre' to concede their demands.

Interference and pressure from within the power hierarchy, wrong policies, procedures, inadequate support from within, vested interests, and incompetence disrupt the power structure. The party system in a democracy has a built in bias towards enlarging the sphere and content of conflict. There exist pockets of incompetence and compartmental decision making. The danger exists that these may multiply and increase in scope and intensity as long as their existing impact on the power structure is not assessed. Political and emotional pressure poses additional threats. They set in motion various demoralizing forces, which in turn affect the power mechanism and its strength.

Corruption further weakens the power structure by forcing shift in power in favor of those who are corrupt. This builds up a zone of vested interests and camp followers demanding more time, energy, and human resources of the power system for negative results. Half-hearted exercise of power weakens the system. Break down of law and order and resulting power losses bring about a shift of power to areas which are detrimental to the national interest. This causes imbalance and further erosion of power.

The absence of a common set of well understood objectives brings about a change in the direction and flow of power. Decision-making is only a process of altering the power flow. The task of the government is only that of managing the elements in the power structure. This is one step farther from that of managing men. The process is a continuous one. Any break in the process intentional or otherwise, necessitates additional set up and start up time merely to regain lost ground.

If government experiments with this scheme of power objectives it will not only act boldly but will achieve rapid economic growth. To be effective its power should be free from adulteration and leakage. The protective sheaths of faith, discipline and hard work can enhance its effectiveness. This is the formula for success. The function of the government is to tap other resources through the use of power. Power objectives have to be related to other objectives of economic growth. If higher levels of leadership assume that only the lower levels have to bear the responsibility for 'power management' failure is a certainty.

Power is a distinct asset of the government. It is to be used as a resource and not as something emotionally attached to and derived from the electorate. It is not a status symbol. The roots of power lie with the people.

The quality of power and its right application decisively determine the quality of life of the people. Elected politicians provide leadership in government. They provide the link between the people and the Executive. Unless these men take positive and dynamic action they will remain as leaders who follow. They must fully equip themselves to discharge their responsibilities by directing the power mechanism. The day they become real leaders motivating followers we shall have 'power management' for economic growth. This calls for development leadership.

3. Motivation
Character and Talent

Motivation

The nation's resources of land, labor, capital and enterprise have to be utilized effectively. Democracy calls for people's participation. The most essential resource required is enterprise, i.e. the ability to take calculated risks for creating wealth. This talent has to be developed and augmented. Leadership can succeed only if it utilizes the reservoir of motivation in individuals whom it leads. This takes us to the need for a new economics for poverty alleviation.

The role of the State will be to generate opportunities so that individuals and institutions are motivated to seize and realize them, thereby increasing employment and output. Undoubtedly the leadership at various levels with the help of the administrative machinery at its disposal is responsible for achieving economic progress. Let us hope it will rise to the occasion to lift the unfortunate millions from the morass of poverty.

Economics is concerned with production and distribution of goods and services ensuring equitable distribution and promoting the welfare of all people. The importance of the subject is realized by all countries and international financing and development agencies. The importance of the subject in promoting human welfare is recognized and Nobel Prize has been instituted in the last half century. Yet there is dissatisfaction among economists, administrators and sections of people over the ineffective manner in which resources are utilized. They are concerned about the prevalence of pockets of poverty with wide disparity in income distribution.

We have come a long way from the days of Adam Smith, passing through the days of Keynesian economics and drawing richly from Welfare economics. But theories and techniques prove to be inadequate to meet the epic challenge of the modern world of rising expectations and complex problems. A solution cannot be considered satisfactory merely in terms of increasing production and national wealth. The most effective means of distribution and that to tackle poverty has to be designed.

Though the importance of the human resource has gained recognition, it has not been utilized to its maximum potential. Refinements of this resource have been taken up in detail under the categories of entrepreneurship and leadership. But even here we are stuck when it comes to poverty alleviation and income distribution. It forces us to think in terms of further refinements in the use of resources and to discover untapped sources.

It is here a penetrating intellect finds a lead towards solution though it may not be perfect and of immediate benefit. In the absence of alternatives we have to give it a trial and make a beginning. This is the area of motivation. The human being, a critical resource, has to be motivated to excel his performance with available and other accessible tools which are least costly. Tools of economics are applied for motivating the human being, to achieve results to reduce disparities in income, to be more productive and to contribute to the growth of the gross domestic product. We shall consider briefly the framework in which this can be accomplished.

The individual is the centre of economic activity. The State is only a catalyst. It has to facilitate the individual to increase productivity and to enrich his contribution to society. For this the State lays down broad targets for increase in gross national product and for reducing disparities in income for poverty alleviation. For this without any bias or prejudice, available sources of knowledge for conservation of resources and increasing their availability with sustainability should be tapped.

Apart from the known resources the reservoir of talent within the individual together with the value system, should be utilized. The government should provide the conditions for developing this input within the individual and facilitate its blooming so that he commands other resources for attaining common objectives. There should not be any shirking of responsibility by the State for resisting and removing hurdles which stand in the way of attaining these objectives.

Our country is a soft state tolerant of wastage, looting, destruction and erosion of resources through channels of corruption and breakdown of law and order.

Widespread agitations by the people and political parties should not be chosen as a way of solving problems or for meeting the objectives. This will require building core competence in the executive, legislature and the judiciary apart from business and industry. The emphasis will be on gaining familiarity with the problems of poverty alleviation and to imbibe unorthodox techniques of character formation on a par with capital formation. The earlier this is attempted the nearer we will be towards a lasting solution.

Here a few lines of explaining the need for motivation are considered relevant. The present tendency of discouraging or even penalizing law abiding citizens and those who take care of themselves with least burden to the State, should give way to motivating them to live a socially useful life and to contribute to the growth of the economy and progress of society.

In a democracy many politicians are catapulted to positions of power by some unusual combination of circumstances. They enjoy a mass base. Many of them lavishly promise to do what they cannot do and what they will not do. But their existence depends on votes. Somehow they command a following. They blindly do what the followers ask and not what is prudent. In this process they mobilize the support of a vast multitude of people who have nothing else to do except creating nuisance of various kinds. Such nuisance includes laying road blocks, setting fire to public transport, holding demonstrations, organizing long processions blocking the entire road, preventing even those who are in dire need of hospitalization reaching their destination and several innumerable acts of nuisance and vandalism. Ultimately public property is damaged and even private property is not spared. Pelting stones is revelry for them. This causes injuries to many. When the police arrive on the scene many of them run away and disappear. The leader is the first to escape. He believes in the escape philosophy practiced successfully. In contrast a law-abiding citizen suffers all harassment. He does not cause any damage to life and property. He pays taxes. But he is put to great misery and agony because of the acts of the vandals. He does not get any incentive to continue his good conduct and behavior. Is he not entitled to get bonus for his good conduct, help in preserving law and order and in helping the government to conserve resources? This is a serious matter which any sane government should consider in public interest.

Economic development is a global objective. All countries want to achieve higher rate of growth to provide citizens higher living standards, national prosperity and a higher quality of life. But have they achieved real progress? Is growth subject to sustainability of resources of all kinds? Has character any role in economic development? We shall briefly consider these aspects and examine the need for any corrective action.

Some countries achieve economic growth at phenomenal rates. The standards of living of their citizens have gone up. At the same time many countries find their growth neutralized by the growing population. They lack access to resources and technology and are unable to command them.

However, there are limits to economic growth. The world's resources are limited and exhaustible over a period of time. So wisdom demands we use them judiciously and develop other resources which will not deplete and which can make a vital contribution to growth with sustainability. We have to identify other resources including intangibles. Just as 'time' has come to be considered as a resource needing proper and productive utilization, why not we consider character as a resource. Why not make a sincere effort to develop it among all citizens so that the whole world benefits substantially.

This has been a serious lacuna in the theory of economic development. Economists talk about labor as a resource or factor of production. But with refinement of this factor through character the results increase many fold. Though at times reference is made to character development, no concerted effort has been made by experts, particularly management and economic professionals. Except for occasional references to value systems no serious research has been done to realize their potential as a resource.

It is laudable to have several Nobel Laureates in economics. But how many have seriously examined the possibility of developing and use of character as a tool of economic development. This will occur to an intelligent mind if it has the will to accept ideas and to apply them. We need not go far to discover it. Already tested tools are available in our ancient scriptures and wisdom.

Character

Economic planning and progress have been unsteady, with exceptions, because of the serious omission to recognize, develop and apply character as a vital input. We now recognize the human being as an important resource. We have so many human resource development programs. We have centers of excellence. But how many centers of character development exist? Huge wastage of resources occurs due to destructive forces and corruption. These can be prevented considerably or their impact minimized by character development.

The primary task for accomplishment of the objective of character development is mind control. This is essential before we impart any serious education. Unfortunately this is totally ignored due to misconceptions and disregard for values. We try hard to control all other resources outside man. But we do not seriously consider the value and potential of the intangible resources within man and to develop and control them for common good. When mind control is attained faculties are better trained and developed through education. This will imbibe qualities of faith, discipline and hard work. Together they ensure success.

Once mind control is achieved technical, human and conceptual skills can be developed rapidly, and with great benefit. It prevents conflicts and even if they occur they are resolved at the earliest stage. Presence of large number of individuals with character will not give room for conflicts. It will eliminate the tendency to be corrupt, and promote mutual help and cooperation. The incidence of criminality and unethical conduct in all areas of human activity, particularly in politics and business, will be considerably reduced. There will be less need for law enforcement and policing, less waste, better distribution of goods and services, well defined priorities, and industrial and social harmony.

It is worth setting up institutions for research and training in character development. Plenty of research material is available from ancient heritage literature and scriptures. We have to take out the principles and make case studies. They have to be made applicable to present day conditions. This is not impossible.

In the same environment men of character have performed exceedingly well without becoming a prey to temptations of any kind. Others succumb to evil influences resulting in wastage of resources. We appeal to the Nobel Laureates, governments and the rich to earmark part of their funds for character development and to pool their brains for achievement in this critical area. The examples and achievements of Japan and Korea should be studied and adopted to suit local needs and conditions.

It is important to remember and ensure that scientific advancement should match with the morality the society can hold. If there is an adverse imbalance it can only bring disastrous results. By character development on a large scale we can avoid this and reduce inequality and global harmony. Every citizen can ponder over these thoughts and do his maximum after convincing himself of the need.

We can achieve the best results from character development. Otherwise we will be creating problems and then trying to find imperfect solutions. Problems of conflict management, stress management, anger management, and probably foolishness management will continue and plague our society.

We go and grasp the root of the malady when we build character. Materialistic economic progress with the best brains cannot solve the problems of mankind and poverty unless character is developed and imparted as an ingredient. Those great souls who gave ancient wisdom made a tremendous contribution to society without expecting anything in return. They had only the welfare of mankind in view. If we do not draw on their wisdom for lasting and sustainable progress we will not succeed. This is something we can say with certainty and which is as certain as death. If we act wisely we will have a wonderful world with a band of devoted individuals dedicated to ensure a better quality of life on this planet.

Problem of sustainability of the human population has been haunting us for long. Population increases take place in economically poor countries depressing living standards. Physical resources are depleted at a faster rate due to economic development and shortages in many sectors appear. The resource crunch leaves its impact on the poor whose basic needs are not met. Poverty stares at them and instability, strife, discontent and disorder have become daily occurrences in many parts of the world.

Resources crunch badly affect those already poor. The inefficiency of the economic system results in misdirected development of the economy driven by market forces and greed and not by need and social justice. More and more resources are diverted to channels producing goods and services catering to the needs of the rich and where profit is high.

The result is that the gap between the rich and the poor is widening. This is seen glaringly after the advent of globalization. The rich command more of purchasing power and more resources of all kinds. This reduces the share of the poor. We see cases of the poor people selling lands which are cornered by the rich. The poor move to remote areas and the steep increase in land prices makes it almost impossible for them to own land and meet their housing needs. Inflation in such countries eats away the purchasing power and renders disposable income insignificant.

Poverty is a dark scar on humanity. It is a source of instability and strife. We cannot wait indefinitely for a solution to this problem. Governments all over the world must have the determination, faith and will to solve it. A time frame is a must but often it cannot be met due to pressure of circumstances. However, we must look for areas where with the available knowledge a solution is possible.

Unfortunately in the name of perverse primitive misconceptions in the name of modernity and secularism value system is neglected by leaders who owe their positions and success due to negation of value systems and wisdom. Instead many of them silently worship criminality and embezzlement. If we see the real factor behind the success of great men who have demonstrated real leadership, we will be convinced they were men of character and their actions were deeply rooted in a rich value system. They derived strength from spirituality. They served the people.

They shook the world facing challenges, overcoming them and lived a life of sacrifice. They enjoyed the happiness arising from a sense of fulfillment. World leaders have to set examples and others in the hierarchy will follow. Thousands of pages can be written on the role of character, values and spirituality in ensuring world prosperity. But what is required is an ounce of practice rather than a ton of talk.

The sooner we act the easier will be our progress towards poverty alleviation. The rich have to take the lead in renouncing the low priority areas in resource utilization. They will do well to release resources or the pressure on resources, to make available essential goods and services for the really poor.

Unless a sincere attempt is made we will continue to bury the problem of poverty under the carpet and poverty abolition will be confined to efforts and talks in five star hotels by brain starved governments. Renunciation of too much enjoyment by all is a must.

The great Greek philosopher Aristotle said twenty-five centuries ago, **"what the world needs is cleansing of hearts and not garments,"** Is this not true even today. We claim to have made lot of progress. Our science and technology have advanced. Our general economic condition has improved. We have more comforts and access to information from any corner of the globe. But with all these and many others, are we really happy? What have we done to improve the lot of the really poor people, exceeding one billion, who are unable to get even one square meal a day? They are not able to acquire minimum education. They don't have a roof over their heads. They have rags on their backs and empty bellies. When they fall sick they do not get the right medical care. Why they should be condemned to a life of penury and misery. Do we, the better off and fortunate among the citizens, have a responsibility to do something within our power to uplift these unfortunate masses?

Everywhere polluted minds exist. They spit venom and spread the contagion of misery and disaster. Even with the most powerful intellect we have not been able to overcome their evil effects. The mightiest nation has not been able to counter their evil designs. The calamity of 9/11 is an example.

Death and destruction in many parts of the globe have become the order of the day. There is wastage of resources. Priorities are lost sight of and in the name of economic development the poor are deprived of their essential requirements for want of resources, or infrastructure, or organizations. We make efforts here and there but they do not make any serious dent on the problem.

It seems there is rise of evil. This brings about competition and waste. Many organizations have a percentage of parasites that take more than what they give. They are more aware of their rights and not duties. Social commitments of organizations are inadequate. Poverty and oppression all over the world, except pockets of wealth and prosperity, do exist. So too is with ignorance and illiteracy.

There are various international funding agencies with programs of poverty eradication but the impact on the poor is slow and negligible. We see countries with booming economy, creating billionaires but the poor live a miserable life as before. Is it not our duty to lift them up from the morass of poverty and despondency? The world economy by and large is greed driven and not by values. The disparity in wealth is increasing. But the large income accruing to the already rich do not find in deployment resources for the welfare of the poor. If the poor around us are in a state of utter want and discontent how can there be stability in society.

Economics deals with satisfaction of human wants. Over a period of time wants become desires and they multiply They are the indiscriminate offspring of the mind .When they are satisfied at the lowest level more and more desires and wants manifest and demand fulfillment. This becomes greed. The nature of greed and its growth is like pouring ghee into fire. The intensity becomes great. When resources are not available to satisfy greed, crooked methods are sought. Greed commands resources and this need not necessarily be based on priority. So resources are cornered by people who perpetuate and promote greed. Though we may call many of them entrepreneurs, many turn out to be thieves of society.

When the tendency to satisfy greed becomes predominant in society such a society adopts all means fair and foul to muster resources. This leads to extensive borrowing since own resources are found to be inadequate. Excessive borrowing creates a situation where repayment of loans becomes difficult and default occurs. This sets in motion a chain reaction and the economy collapses causing fall in employment and rise in economic misery. The lone culprit is greed.

Thus the bane of society is greed and if we want to improve society and its economic condition we must curb greed. Greed results in wastage of resources. The recent stock market crash and global meltdown confirm this phenomenon.

The global melt down of the last decade had its origin in human greed which prompted individuals to acquire assets even at the risk of heavy borrowing. Banks welcomed borrowers to further their business. This led to business boom and later a bubble burst. We are yet to recover from the onslaught of this big hit. Share markets crashed. Banks collapsed .This resulted in loss of millions of jobs. Loss of income caused proliferation of misery. Economic theory based on multiplicity of desires and wants can only offer a faulty structure wIth loose foundation.

Are not resources cornered and wasted? Are there not priorities for human existence? Why not upgrade human values which will definitely scale down greed and ensure better standards of living for all instead of extreme happiness for a few and acute misery for many. Controlling greed is the function of controlling the mind with the power of the intellect. If our educational system can achieve this in a decade steadily we will definitely march towards stable progress without tears. Let us start building up a global value system relinquishing greed. Let us not salute greed as an engine of economic progress.

While greed dominates economic order, spiraling inflation demolishes the hopes of any progress for the poor. Disorder and discontent become their constant companions. There is unhappiness due to lack of essential things for their use. There is unhappiness for the rich due to a feeling of insecurity for the protection of their life and property. Is this state of tension, stress and anxiety desirable? How can we get over this?

How long should this continue? Is it not time to end this? Efforts of several agencies like the World Bank, Asian Development Bank yield some results but they are inadequate.

Poverty cannot be abolished by the efforts of persons who travel in executive class and live in five star hotel and comforts. They should really understand the problems of the poor. They should feel for them and live poverty at least for a while to understand the intensity of the malady. Human relationships should be based on love and helping the others. It should not be brushed aside as pure philosophy or impractical ideal. In fact the idealist is the most practical man in the world. He raises the level of practicality to the ideal and does not pull down the ideal to the low level of practicality. There is need for a supra ordinary goal of human welfare and happiness with focus on programs for the really poor. We must go back to Gandhian values and our ancient wisdom which ensured social security without state intervention.

We have to mould a new generation if the present one cannot accomplish or attune to this. We should stop this plunder of resources by a section of rich and fortunate ones who in the name of progress are driven by greed instead of need. Programs of education and skill development should tap the mental strength of mankind and tap the heart for the inexhaustible fountain of love. This alone can provide a lasting solution for world peace, prosperity, happiness and stability. This should be done with the full participation of the really poor that will benefit. Globalization of values is the need of the times. This is the task of global and national leadership. Our efforts during all these centuries have been the result of application of the intelligence to solve man's problems. But have we solved them fully? Are we confident that they will be solved with the intellect alone? Is there a better way open to us? It is here Aristotle's statement becomes more relevant today. Let us make a beginning now. Thus we can pay a glowing tribute to Aristotle and his maxim. Let us pray wisdom will dawn on our leaders who profess to be champions of poverty alleviation.

Talent

Progress is the function of good leadership and talents. Leaders should locate talents within their areas of responsibility and influence. This has to be a continuous process. The right leadership is welcomed by talented individual to make contributions to society.

We all know what talent means. This is a natural skill or ability at something. It comes to people in diverse ways. Some people are lucky to live out the full potential of their talents; some others discover their talents but are not privileged enough to harness them; while yet another group live and die without ever knowing what their real talents are. In any community there will be at least one person who is very good in at least one activity. It might be somebody known to us or not.

Ideally we might hope that society would reward people having talent. The person with ability to do a particular activity would go on to use that ability to his and society's advantage. That is perfectly logical.

But often we find that people with talent are not allowed to use that talent and frustration develops. More than this society as a whole loses the advantages of having the best people employed in positions best suited to them.

We need good economy to harness creative talents and we need harnessed talents to create good economy. We have to develop a synergy between the already developed talents and the government in order to harness more talents. Society should learn from the mistakes of that generation that mismanaged creativity and do better

There are many young men and women in our society today who need capital to launch one enterprise or the other. There should be a synergy between the government and philanthropists to empower creative youths.

Leaders at various levels should take seriously such projects as job centers, creativity village, skill acquisition, and organizations that promote creativity. These, shall in turn contribute to build a strong and stable economy where creative empowerment and social development will be a way of life. We must learn to discover and promote creative talents wherever they are.

The only way is to originate solutions from the heart of human beings. Where intellect fails the heart succeeds, the heart of the Buddha with overflowing compassion for the unfortunate ones. Out of that compassion springs forth spontaneous release of resources from individuals. This alone can solve the problem of poverty and misery. There will be less for governmental intervention. Let us fill every heart with values. This does not mean the present functions discharged by the governments should be discarded or given less importance. In addition make human hearts overflow with concern and compassion for releasing resources and energy for the uplift of the really poor. A civilization worth the name should really progress in cleansing the hearts. It is a heart full with values, which will be the springboard of love. Noble action and programs for the uplift of the poor will follow. This needs a global view.

4. Development Leadership

The basic problem facing a poor country is the inability of leadership to launch fruitful programs and to carry the masses along with them. Although rare cases of efficiency at top levels of leadership do exist, they are inadequate to meet the challenges and magnitude of the problems. Leadership, which walks on stilts, cannot make significant progress towards poverty abolition.

Actions of leaders both in power and in the opposition have contributed towards inflating the needs of the people and depleting the nation's resources. Any program of leadership development must achieve the basic requirements of the people with reference to these two arms of poverty i.e. needs and resources. The purpose here is not to discuss the techniques of developing leadership. Our focus of attention is only on what is immediately needed for abolition of poverty. The span of vision required by leaders can thus be narrowed down to two areas. These are:

1.   To reduce the needs of the affluent population to basic necessities, essential articles and services and to conserve resources.

2.   *To devise and develop various techniques suited to local conditions and implement* them to attain results in the area of poverty abolition.

Three elements are hostile to the realization of these objectives. One is the increasing materialistic attitude of the people fanned by desires to imitate the affluent sections of society. Another is the disrespect for law and order displayed by many sections of population including many levels of leadership. The third element is corruption by men in responsible positions. The first one inflates the needs of individuals and thus distorts the demand. The second and third result in erosion of resources. According to a research report by Global Financial Integrity, India lost Rs 28 lakh crores in illicit outflows during 2003 -2012 on account of corruption, bribery and kickbacks, criminal activities and efforts to shelter wealth from the country's tax authorities. This amount could wipe out India's external debt and leave crores for poverty alleviation. Thus there is pressing the need for plugging leakages through corruption.

Widespread destruction of property and productive resources during a countrywide agitation results in loss amounting to crores of rupees. It is easy to destroy wealth, property and resources of such a magnitude in a few days. But it takes several months' effort, financial and technical assistance, for reconstruction of lost facilities and many years to recoup the loss completely. In the context of the state undertaking the responsibility for major economic activity, even a modest rate of five percent 'corruption allowance' depletes the resources considerably.

The three enemies of poverty referred to earlier, demand qualities of leadership deeply rooted in values and supported by our cultural heritage. Such qualities include austerity, non-violence and integrity. Austerity helps to curtail non priority needs. An attitude of non-violence enables one to seek solutions through ways other than loss of productive resources. Integrity enables one to withstand corruptive influences. These three qualities, which constitute the antidote to poverty, are crystallized in the concept of character.

Though they are needed in all citizens, these qualities are essential for leaders. Without them leadership will never be able to lead and inspire the masses. Such a leadership will be non-performing. Any program of leadership development must stress the need and methods for development of these qualities. Basic values have to be culled out, codified and imbibed. Only a leadership deeply rooted in such values and living by example can have great impact on the followers. The masses are inspired to emulate their example. Under such conditions corruptive influences lose their hold and there is greater conservation and productive use of resources.

A comprehensive leadership development program has to be evolved. This requires training of leaders and those individuals with potential. The objective of the training program should be:

• To train leaders at different levels of activity
• To provide essential background required for a national perspective and
• To develop skills in solving problems.

The training is solely for developing leadership to achieve economic growth on right lines. The different levels determined geographically are only classifications for administrative convenience. Objectives could be achieved through a training program spread over a period of four years. The duration could be varied according to the level of leadership.

According to World Bank reports about two-thirds of India's people depend on rural employment for a living. Going forward, it will be essential for India to build a productive, competitive, and diversified agricultural sector and facilitate rural, non-farm entrepreneurship. Encouraging policies that promote competition in agricultural marketing will ensure that farmers receive better prices. This takes us to the need for rural development.

The level of inequality has risen high. Hunger in India has reached its highest level in decades. Any attempt at rural development must give priority to tackle the problem of rural poverty, Unemployment is extensive.

Development programs have not left much impact in the rural areas.

For development of rural Intensive Development Centers, resources could be raised in many ways. One source is the government, which makes allocations for various territories under the national plans or area development programs. We can determine the adequacy or inadequacy of funds provided for executing the programs. Apart from this source, public and private firms in proximity to the IDCs could be approached and motivated to provide assistance. They could finance directly some programs or depute trained personnel in different fields to administer the programs.

For such services the government could compute the cost and give tax exemptions. This should be considered as encouraging social responsibility of business. The inflow of remittance from outside should be considered for determining total financial assistance required for the Centre. This requires an organization to prepare plans and detailed programs of implementation for each IDC. A proper mix of unemployed graduates and trained personnel could man these centers guided by experienced hands that will cover a cluster of ten (or a viable number) centers under their jurisdiction. IDCs of ten will form a Regional Development Centre. Coordination will be effected at each of the administrative centers (RDCs and ZDCs) with the centers in charge of urban development and other government agencies at a higher level.

Simultaneous action will be taken by the urban development department in each city to decongest territories witnessing overcrowding and excessive development. This will be a continuous process. Any decongestion move will be based on study of flow of people from the rural or suburban areas to the city for such services. A study determining the extent to which the services could be dispersed will precede this. After study of the flow of people from each area to the city, schools, colleges, hospitals, government offices, etc. could be dispersed. This will also help to reduce the strain on the transportation system. Purchasing power will get diffused in the suburban areas and gradually percolate into the rural areas.

The success of the program of IDCs needs an effective organization. At the IDC level this will be located within the IDC, as far as possible. For a group of IDCs the entire task of rural development will be considered as a total system. Objectives to ensure all round development of IDCs to attain a minimum level of per capita income will be laid down. While the IDC organization will be the primary agency to plan, implement and monitoring, the inputs and the logistics support will be provided by various agencies constituting the subsystems. These are: inputs procuring agency, public/private sector firms, and social/ voluntary organizations, private individuals/cooperatives within the IDCs, government agencies, output marketing agency, banks and post offices. The last two are concerned with mobilizing external remittances coming to the people in the IDC area. The data will be helpful to determine the availability of funds within the IDC from people's own resources.

The IDC will define the system objectives with reference to the minimum requirements of the area. This will be within the broad framework of the policy for rural development to fulfill considerations of national interest. The system objectives could be:

1.   *To generate average purchasing power to exceed the per capita income of the territory, and to double it in five years*

2.   *To provide employment at least to one able bodied member from each family*

3.   *To increase productivity of the resources in the IDC area*

4.   *To provide or supplement the expertise available in the IDC area for attainment of objectives.*

5.   *To provide the inputs necessary for attainment of IDC program and*

6.   *To set up industrial and agro processing units which will utilize local resources*

Successful attainment of system objectives requires objectives for the various subsystems, which are illustrated below:

The Inputs Procuring Agency will have to determine the adequacy and extent of input availability within the IDC area, the quantum, timing and nature of input to ensure availability of such inputs and to prepare detailed input budgets.

The corporate and commercial organizations will have objectives to determine the number of IDCs that could be taken up for intensive care and assistance, the nature and assistance to be given, the type and number of experts to be provided and their duration, training needs of the IDCs and devise ways to meet them and to provide financial assistance to the IDCs.

The objectives of social and voluntary organizations will be to determine the area within the IDC where effective service could be rendered, to provide trained personnel for the task to be undertaken by the IDC, and to mobilize funds for production needs within the IDC.

Government agencies form another sub system. They will set objectives to provide all assistance and support required for IDCs, to coordinate with RDCs and ZDCs and to avoid overlapping functions. They will also determine the extent of deficit in inputs including finance and take corrective measures, It will be their responsibility to determine the impact of decongestion (de-urbanization) programs and to locate pockets of poverty and in cooperation with the RDCs and ZDCs evolve programs for implementation.

Commercial banks will have to recast their objectives for lending to IDCs. The present policy of micro enterprise financing will have to be extended on a large scale. Similar objectives will be necessary for other institutions concerned with financing and training of personnel for IDCs. Another subsystem, the marketing and distributing agency, will set objectives to market output generated and to ensure economic price realization.

The strategy for rural development for poverty alleviation has unique features. It does not approach the problems of rural development in isolation or piecemeal. It minimizes chances of occurrence of pockets of undeveloped areas. It is village oriented and attempts development of an intensive development centre- IDC, from within and by promoting a wave of de-urbanization. The two-pronged attack with a systems approach with various coordinated subsystems will ensure all round development, which could be accelerated or regulated as per need. It is worth implementing this idea at least in a few territories. This will help to assess the operational difficulties if any and to improve it before implementing it over a larger area. In fact, this is the strategy towards which leadership in poor countries should move, act and succeed. The Unique Identity System and information technology will help to accomplish the objectives rapidly.

The program can include the following subjects:

- Character and economic development
- Constitution
- Cultural and religious forces
- Decision-making
- Environment of the country
- Factors promoting economic development
- Factors retarding economic growth
- Fiscal policy and banking policy

- International economic situation
- Management of resources
- Monetary system and economic growth
- Motivation and productivity
- National objectives/policies/strategies
- Planning and implementation
- Prices, productivity and output
- Problems in administration
- Quantitative techniques in decision-making
- Science and economic growth

The program can richly draw from the experience of various developing countries, which have successfully managed their economies. Contemporary economic events could be chosen for analysis. Emphasis will be on saving cost, time and effort in attaining results. Continuous research will be necessary to revise the syllabus to reflect the latest experience and problems of such countries. It could be a four tier program involving different but related levels of leadership. Economic development is not merely the result of financial and technical assistance. It has to be achieved through effective management of society through quality leadership.

The training and development proposed should be based on observations of problems of sick as well as growing economies and their solutions. Protests and demonstrations cannot attain objectives. As Prof. Samuelson has observed, "slogans of socialism or banners, and constitutions are not sufficient to promote rapid industrial progress."

The national government is primarily responsible for economic development. But advanced countries could devise productive ways of economic assistance e.g., a package for creation of infrastructure facilities in a specific territory consisting of a group of villages. These are elementary education, secondary education, health, social security, energy, water, transport, power, roads, railways, ports, transportation systems and effective service delivery

Initially this could be implemented on an experimental basis. The current thinking in business points to greater awareness of the Corporate Social Responsibility. Tie up with large corporate business houses will provide social entrepreneurship, professional inputs and resources to achieve the objective of poverty reduction. Such assistance will keep in view the objective of generating leadership all over the territory.

The core of the programs will be to stress the need for developing an attitude that will reflect that:

- A sense of urgency and regard for time is essential for progress.
- Breakdown of law and order destroys resources
- Corruption accentuates poverty.
- Employment is meaningful only if it is productive.
- Improvement in the quality of life of citizens is the concern of leadership
- Motivation and productivity are essential for removing poverty
- Production is as important as distribution.
- Promoting the welfare of the unorganized masses and those below the poverty level deserves top priority
- Taxation is to be used as a motivating tool
- The role of the State is to create opportunities for advancement of citizens and
- Values are important for progress

Leadership development in the long run has to come from a change in education policy. This should concentrate on changing the attitudes of citizens for the better. It should focus on creating attitudes that will achieve efficiency, diligence, orderliness, punctuality, frugality, honesty, rationality, integrity and self-reliance. It should also create in them preparedness for change and alertness to opportunities. Many who really take education seriously find the tentacles of misery and despondency coiling on them. They seize the earliest opportunity to seek jobs outside the country. Advanced countries provide assistance and training to persons in poor countries. Ultimately they benefit by having the services of trained persons who end up in serving them.

If a breakthrough is to be made for a solution to the problem of poverty, it is essential that this trend be reversed. Research activity in educational institutions must concentrate on the areas of motivation, values and economic progress. Undoubtedly importance has to be given to character development. The relationship between character and economic development should be recognized and programs designed to form a practical course module in this area. In addition areas chosen should include improvement of law and order and elimination of corruption. This calls for an institutional approach.

Thus the key instrument for abolition of poverty is development leadership. Quality leadership reinforced by a well-educated population sharpens it. It strengthens national and individual character through setting examples. The benefits of education, though slow and time consuming, will be steady and lasting. Quality leadership and sound education interact. Character formation has a multiplier effect. It also accelerates capital formation by assisting conservation of resources and thus promotes economic growth and abolition of poverty.

It is relevant here to remember the following words of Swami Vivekananda.

"So long as the millions live in hunger and ignorance, I hold every person a traitor who, having been educated at their expense pays not the least heed to them".

In the task of poverty abolition, the rich have a positive role. Many among them have been pace setters. They enjoy high standards of living, which imply a varied and more complex hierarchy of needs. As mentioned earlier one arm of poverty is the growing need hierarchy. The rich are achieving higher levels of living and the poor are unable to maintain even their existing levels. In this context the view expressed by the famous economist and Nobel Laureate Jan Tin Bergen is of great significance.

This view of the Nobel Laureate deserves serious consideration by all agencies, national and international, concerned with poverty abolition. If there is one thing certain and is badly needed, it is the development and cultivation of a value system which alone can impart strength and stability to any solution. Great leaders have shown the way. We have to follow them and look for areas for further improvement. Then only we can remove poverty from the face of this planet.

5. Social Security

The world is in the grip of the globalization phenomenon. Billionaires are increasing in thousands. At the same time there are billions of poor who cannot afford two square meals a day, let alone the necessities of civilized life. There is no social security cover for most of them.

India adopted a constitution declaring the country to be a Sovereign Democratic Republic guaranteeing to all its citizens equality of opportunity, and justice, economic and social. The real prosperity of a country is indicated by the extent of social security provided to its citizens, employment, health care, living standards, quality of life and dignity of citizens. So far social security for under privileged population on a national scale has not been thought of seriously by the governments. The fear that grips the leaders in government is that resources of huge magnitude cannot be found. It is here a change in approach to the problem and its solution is necessary. Where resources constraints exist priorities are a must. The poorest of the poor, the bottom 20.6% in the below poverty level section of the population have to be identified. This can be in terms of their geographical spread and basic needs.

It is tragic and an irony of fate that in a country with 20.6 of the population below the poverty line, compensation for rise in prices is given at regular intervals as allowances to some sections of society who are affluent .This equals the salary after a few years. It is also painful to see that every five years salaries are revised for all categories of government servants .The arrears come to a heavy amount and accrue as a windfall. This creates a situation that the government has to incur additional burden of Rs.20000 crores annually

The logic is strange indeed. If inflation justifies increasing the level of compensation for those having a decent income far above the subsistence level, nothing need be provided for those who do not have even the means of getting one meal a day. It implies seeing some men as human beings and others as human pigs. This thinking does not fit in with the values of a civilized society claiming to be progressive.

The immediate task before any democracy is not merely to get better results within the existing framework of economic and social institutions. It is to mould and recondition these institutions so that they contribute effectively to the realization of wider and deeper values. The Indian government has given stress to values by incorporating them in the Directive Principles of State Policy. These are fundamental in the governance of the country. It shall be the duty of the State to apply these principles in making laws. The State shall try to promote the welfare of the people by securing and making as effectively as it may a social order in which justice, social, economic and political, shall inform all the institutions of national life (Art.38). It shall in particular direct its policy toward securing:

i that all citizens, men and women, equally, have the right to an adequate means of livelihood

ii. that the ownership and control of the material resources of the community are so distributed as best to serve the common good;

iii. that the operation of the economic system does not result in the concentration of wealth and means of production to the common detriment (Art.39)

In pursuance of the contents of these principles it is imperative that the resources of the corporate sector, including the public sector, should be utilized for giving relief to the poor. To make a beginning, as a measure of social security for the really poor, those below the poverty line, and unemployed adults could be considered as target groups. This is the edifice on which anti poverty efforts of the future is to be built. The social security proposed is a concept which provides for a minimum regular income to poor citizens below the BPL. This includes the unemployed above 18, enabling all to ward off starvation using social security plank as the base and to strive for further progress.

Basic needs in terms of food, clothing, shelter, health and education have to be met.

Everywhere economic growth is worshipped as the most laudable objective. These efforts are supplemented by the contributions of international agencies like the World Bank and the Asian Development Bank.

In spite of all these efforts the problem of poverty poses a perennial challenge and it still raises its ugly head. The growth in national income and per capita income is rendered insignificant. The galloping inflation and growing population in many countries often neutralize it. This trend is aggravated by the scarcity of some essential goods and services.

Government is the fountainhead of power, which is manifested through policies and strategies at various levels. The role of government in a scheme of poverty eradication should be to motivate the affluent sections of society to transfer surplus resources to the poor and to provide the necessary administrative framework and infrastructure through legislative and executive action. Its important asset is power, which has to be treated as a resource and used as a lever to influence the behavior of all other resources.

In a democracy this resource of power is vested in the elected representatives of the people. It takes various forms. The Executive, Legislature and the Judiciary exercise it. These institutions have to use it in a coordinated manner for poverty eradication.

This calls for poverty abolition objectives at the global level by international agencies. This should not be confined to economic objectives only. Any area of human activity which will help to solve the problem should be considered for evolving objectives. Broadly the objectives could cover the following areas.

Conservation of resources: This can be achieved by preventing waste and leakage of resources.

Increasing productivity of resources: This can be attained by improving techniques, methods, practices.

Allocating priorities: This can be attained by allocating more resources to produce goods and services to meet the basic necessities of the poor people.

Sustainability of population, environment, and resources: This can be achieved by persistent efforts at educating the people.

Use of available wisdom handed over through ages: Here values have a very vital role. This is least expensive, pollution free and always has a conserving impact and influence. Character has a very great role in promoting economic development. This is the least expensive but most effective tool for development. It is deeply rooted in the value system and wisdom we have inherited over the ages.

The failure of democracy to make significant progress in the areas of poverty abolition is due to the failure of leadership to conserve and canalize power and to use it as catalyst for development activity that can substantially benefit the poor. Thus the problem of poverty has to be tackled in the area of leadership.

Poor countries do not have as many problem solving leaders as problem creating ones. The latter mislead the masses and their actions result in considerable wastage of resources. The answer to the question of poverty lies in the creation of a society in which such perilous deception of the unthinking masses is no longer possible. High quality leadership with the will to solve problems alone can achieve this.

6. Epilogue

Anti poverty measures call for immediate action. Our emphasis is on leadership development which we have discussed in some detail in earlier chapters. Action by leadership in power, in the opposition, the people within the country and by the rich nations is necessary. This is summarized below.

Leadership in Power

1.   Set up a Ministry for Poverty Alleviation

2.   Consider impact of action taken under various schemes in favor of organized sections on unorganized sections of labor
3.   Create a well integrated power network based on systems approach
4.   Create opportunities for employment
5.   Develop power management objectives
6.   Develop problem solving approach
7.   Discard craze for privileges
8.   Discourage problem creating leaders
9.   Do not make promises and rapidly wear them out
10.   Encourage enterprise and talent

11.   Encourage productive employment
12.   Firmly maintain law and order
13.   Focus attention on areas of immediate returns ,and order base and rooting out corruption
14.   Give up the implicit policy of being a soft state
15.   Improve quality of life
16.   Inculcate discipline
17.   Look constantly for disruption in power structure and take corrective action
18.   Manage power effectively
19.   Motivate people
20.   Realize the power potential of the administration
21.   Reduce inequality of opportunity
22.   Set clear anti-poverty objectives
23.   Use tax system as a motivating tool

Opposition

1.   Hold on to anti-poverty objectives
2.   Help government to realize anti poverty objectives
3.   Do not disrupt the power structure
4.   Do not stifle enterprise
5.   Do not stall legislative proceedings
6.   Impart discipline and decorum in dealings
7.   Do not demoralize those working for increased output, productivity and employment

8. Do not constrict opportunity
9. Do not cause wastage of resources by encouraging breakdown of law and order

10. Do not disrupt value systems
11. Give up problem creating approach
12. Improve quality of life

The People

1. Choose right leaders who will deliver positive results
2. Develop individual objectives consistent with national objectives

Rich Nations

1. Be pace setters in simpler ways of living
2. Create infrastructure in group of villages with stress on generating quality leadership
3. Ensure sustainability of resources
4. Focus assistance on education
5. Promote development leadership;
6. Set anti poverty objective in the world context
7. Step up contributing to poverty alleviation programs

In addition to action on these lines the state has to change its role. Its function should be to create opportunities for improving the quality of life of citizens.

Poverty is a painful experience. It arises from many causes, the most important being poverty of right leadership. This has been attested by great world leaders. There is considerable scope for improvement through clear anti poverty objectives which also require leadership objectives. This requires effective 'power management'. The role of power is to motivate the people and not to regulate their freedom indiscriminately curbing initiative and enterprise. Rich nations can render considerable help by providing assistance for development leadership. We can learn a lot from countries like Sri Lanka in the area of poverty alleviation and leadership development.

Democracy should not mean a surfeit of freedom for the leaders and people to do anything they like so that 'the horse begins to drive the wayfarer from the road'. What the country in particular and the world in general need today is cleansing of hearts and not of garments. Emphasis should be laid on character development which is a highly productive intangible asset. Such an approach to the nation's problems by the leaders and the lead will pave the way for the elimination of poverty. There is enough for our present day leaders in all walks of life to learn from our ancient scriptures, which have as much relevance today as it was in the distant past.

Our vision in India is to make India a great place to work. Such a lofty vision cannot be achieved by a group of mediocre, uninspired individuals posing as leaders. The sheer magnitude of the vision makes it necessary that we attract inspired people who are not just talented in the ordinary sense of having outstanding competencies, but deeply passionate about making a difference. Such a leadership alone can eliminate poverty and usher in prosperity.

End of Vol. 2

•